Collins

Cherry Blossoms

English

UKG

FS3

SERIES EDITOR: RANI THIPPAVAZZULA

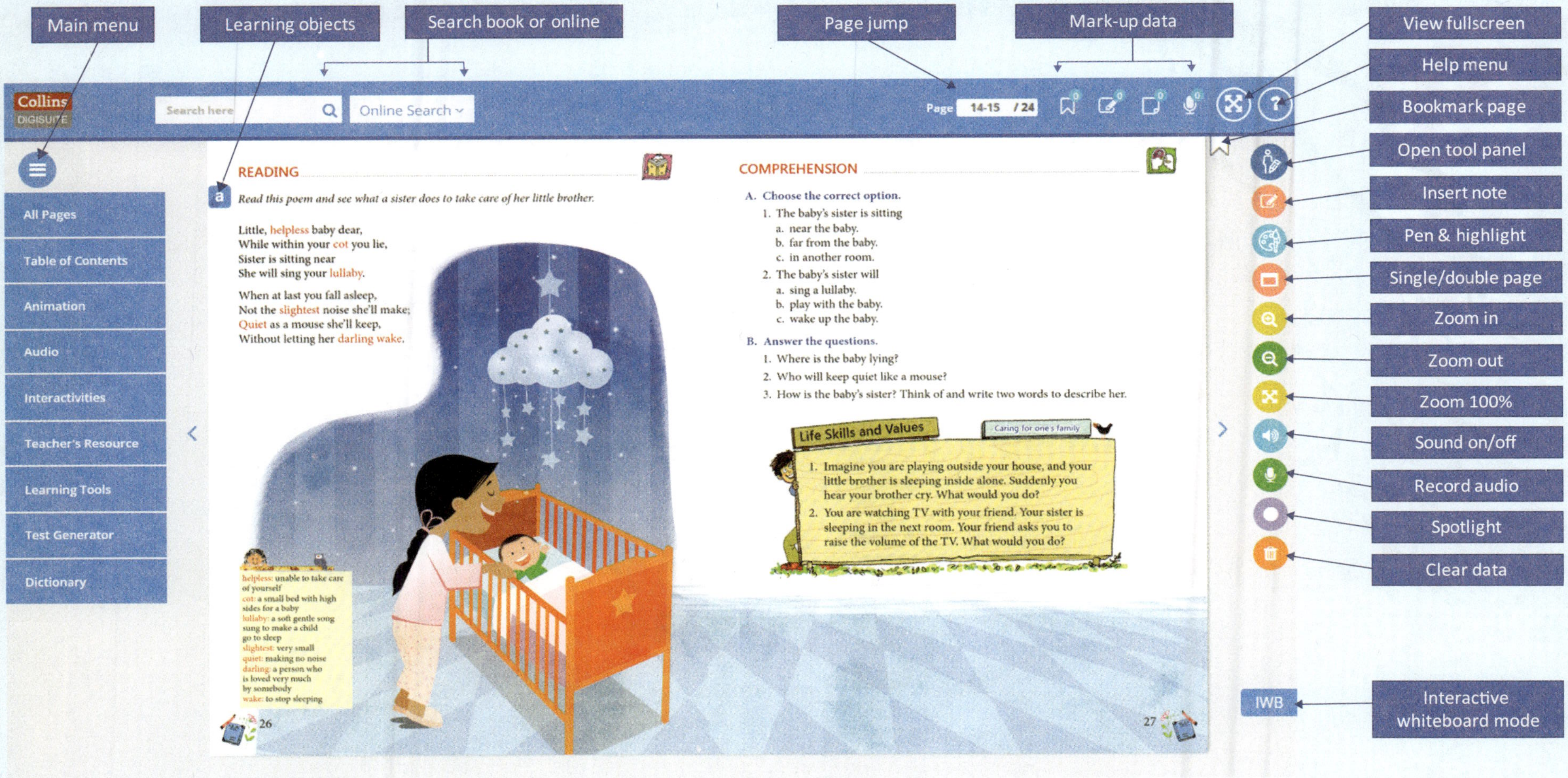

Student + Teacher			Teacher-only	
a animations	**ia** activities	**g** games	**lp** lesson plans	**tn** teacher's notes
ilt instructor-led tutorials	**w** worksheets	**v** videos	**w** worksheets	**ak** answer keys
	audio			

Preface

Cherry Blossoms provides graded, age-appropriate learning opportunities targeting holistic skill development for children in the age group of 3 years to 8 years. The series aligns with the vision outlined in the National Education Policy, 2020 for early years. It spreads across five levels, Nursery (Foundational Stage 1) to Class 2 (Foundational Stage 5). The books use a combination of hands-on activities, frequent recapitulation and child-friendly artwork to facilitate learning.

The series comprises **40 books** and spans **English**, **Maths**, **General Awareness**, and **Art and Craft**. The series comes bundled with a **workbook** for each subject and a book of **rhymes** and **stories** for Foundational Stage 1 to 3.

This series integrates the essence of **NIPUN Bharat** guidelines, which extensively deal with Foundational Literacy and Numeracy. The series aims to motivate learners to read independently, to improve their vocabulary, number sense and spatial understanding. The **Foundational Literacy and Numeracy (FLN)** skills include the skills for developing their critical thinking, logical reasoning and creative skills, as well as the skills to enhance their ability to express themselves both verbally and in writing.

Cherry Blossoms Teacher Support Materials include:

Teacher's Resource Books: Comprises stories, activity banks, classroom management and assessment guidelines

Multimedia eBook: Consists of animations, audio, video, slide shows, and interactive exercises

Print-ready Worksheets: Additional worksheets for practice and reinforcement, present in the digital support

Digital Flashcards: Flashcards with embedded sounds and animations for letter formation and letter-sound association

Animations and Songs: Animated stories and rhymes set to tune

Interactive Games: Interactivities to reinforce concepts in a fun and engaging manner

A note on the activity banks (included in the Teacher's Manuals)

The activity banks comprise hands-on activities that will help children develop the requisite skills to attain age-appropriate learning goals. In keeping with Howard Gardener's theory of multiple intelligences, the activity banks include options and variations that enable teachers to provide a planned cycle of experiences and opportunities, which foster each type of intelligence, to every child in their classrooms. The activity banks equip teachers to use the strengths of children as a means of complementing their less developed areas by valuing and nurturing the inherent abilities of the children.

Rani Thippavazzula, former Academic Director, Ravindra Bharathi Group is an eminent educationist with over two decades of experience in teaching, administration and curriculum design and development. As an Academic Advisor for chain schools pan India, she is proficient in developing learning products and is a specialist in Differentiated Instruction, Enterprise Education and Early Childhood Education.

Learning and Development During the Early Years

The early years are the most significant years for growth, development and learning. During this period, children need adequate opportunities for stimulating experiences as these favourably affect various learning abilities. Learning experiences, when chosen and planned properly, fuel the innate curiosity of children, and stimulate their thought processes.

The goal of learning during the early years is to enhance the all-round development of personality and to inculcate healthy attitudes, life skills and good values. Creative play, well thought-out games and developmentally appropriate activities help children develop the necessary skills to achieve these goals. The skills that children need to acquire can broadly be categorized as:

Motor:
Motor skills pertain not only to gross motor activities like walking and jumping but also include fine motor activities like the ability to hold a pencil and write. The development of motor skills is facilitated through several graded activities.

Personal, Social and Emotional:
Personal, social and emotional development, necessary for the overall personality development of children, is achieved using a combination of hands-on activities, role plays and thought-provoking stories and rhymes.

Linguistic:
The ability to listen, speak, read and write is critical to success in formal learning environments.

Mathematical:
The development of mathematical ideas and concepts is important at this stage since children will continue to build on this learning for most of their years of schooling.

Knowledge and Understanding of the World:
This is achieved through activities that enable children to explore their surroundings at home and in the school, and interact with the people that they see around them.

Health and Safety: The idea of health and safety is introduced through activities, stories and retelling of real-life experiences to encourage children to focus on health and well-being.

Creative:
Creative skills are developed through a host of activities involving art, craft, painting, roleplays, etc.

Logical and Rational Thinking:
Activities that involve simple puzzles, pattern-completion and visual discrimination help children to develop logical and rational thinking skills.

Contents

Letters of the Alphabet 8
I Know the Letters of the Alphabet....12
Hello Letters Aa and Bb....................13
Hello Letters Cc and Dd 14
I Know Letters Aa–Dd.......................15
Hello Letters Ee and Ff......................16
Hello Letters Gg and Hh....................17
I Know Letters Ee–Hh.......................18
Hello Letters Ii and Jj.......................19
Hello Letters Kk and Ll......................20
I Know Letters Ii–Ll..........................21
Hello Letters Mm and Nn 22
Hello Letters Oo and Pp....................23
I Know Letters Mm–Pp.......................24
Hello Letters Qq and Rr 25
Hello Letters Ss and Tt......................26
I Know Letters Qq–Tt........................27
Hello Letters Uu and Vv 28
Hello Letters Ww and Xx...................29
Hello Letters Yy and Zz 30
I Know Letters Uu–Zz.........................31
I Know This–That! 32
I Know Where You Hide! 34
Introduction to One–Many................36
I Know one and many things!............37
Introduction to These–Those.............39
I Know These–Those Things! 40
I Know What You Do! 42
Dobby and His Friends 44
Question Words 46
I Know! 48
I Know Sight Words!..........................50
Reading Words (short vowel 'a' words) 52
I Know! 53
I Can Write Words! 54
Reading Words (short vowel 'e' words)..55
I Know! 56
I Can Read 57
Reading Words (short vowel 'i' words) 58
I Know! 59
I Can Write Words! 60
Reading Words (short vowel 'o' words) 61
I Know! 62
I Can Write Words! 63
Reading Words (short vowel 'u' words) 64
I Know! 65
I Can Read 66
Introduction to A/An 68
Magic 'e' 70
Introduction to Yes/No 72
Reading More Words 74
I Know! 80
Introduction to And............................84
The Fox and the Crane 87
I Can Read! 88
I Know! 95
Opposites 98
I Can Read (repeated consonants)...100
Lazy Tom 101
I Know! 102
Rhyme Along 108
I Know! 109
Goldilocks and The Three Bears 110
Jumbled Words 111
Introduction to Sentences 113
Guided Sentence Writing................114
Guided Sentence Writing Yes/No 115
Guided Sentence Writing................116
I Can Read and Write 118

WALKTHROUGH

HELLO LETTERS Kk and Ll

Read the words.

kitten kettle kangaroo Kk kite king

Trace and write k.

Read the words.

lad log ladder Ll lip lid leg lap

Trace and write l.

Writing of lower case letters covered. The emphasis is on strengthening letter–sound association and encouraging little learners to read three-letter words independently

READING WORDS (SHORT VOWEL 'a' WORDS)

Point and read.

-ab cab tab -ad lad sad

-ag bag rag tag -an fan pan

-ap cap lap map tap

-at bat cat hat rat

52

Reading of words with short and long vowel sounds, consonant blends and digraphs, repeated consonants

I CAN READ (REPEATED CONSONANTS)

Point and read.

-all ball small fall tall

-ill ill pill drill bill

-ell bell tell yellow

-oll roll -ull bull

-ss grass glass mess kiss

-rr cherry strawberry

100

DOBBY AND HIS FRIENDS

Look at the pictures. Talk about each picture.

44

Read about Dobby, Rob and Leena.

Hello! I am Dobby.

I like to eat and.

This is Rob.

is my friend.

He likes to eat and.

He shares his treats with me.

This is Leena.

She and are friends.

She likes to eat.

She gets for me.

What do you like to eat? Draw

MAGIC 'e'

Sing.

Let me teach you a game

Magic e is my name

Add me to any word...

abracadabra...

Hear the vowel say its name.

Name the pictures. Add the magic e. Read the words.

tap + e → tape

fin + e → fine

tub + e → tube

bit + e → bite

can + e → cane

man + e → mane

70

Rhymes and stories used to introduce and reinforce concepts

Stories to support social and emotional development, emphasize basic values, develop creative thinking and language skills

Revision activities in a variety of formats to keep it interesting and challenging for little learners

Writing-based revision pages to further fine motor development

LETTERS OF THE ALPHABET

Trace the letters with your finger. Say the letters aloud. Name the pictures.

Aa

Bb

Cc

Dd

Ee

Ff

Gg

Hh

Ii

Jj

Kk

Ll

Mm

Nn

LETTERS OF THE ALPHABET

Trace the letters with your finger. Say the letters aloud. Name the pictures.

Uu

Vv

Ww

Xx

Yy

Zz

I KNOW THE LETTERS OF THE ALPHABET

Write the missing letters.

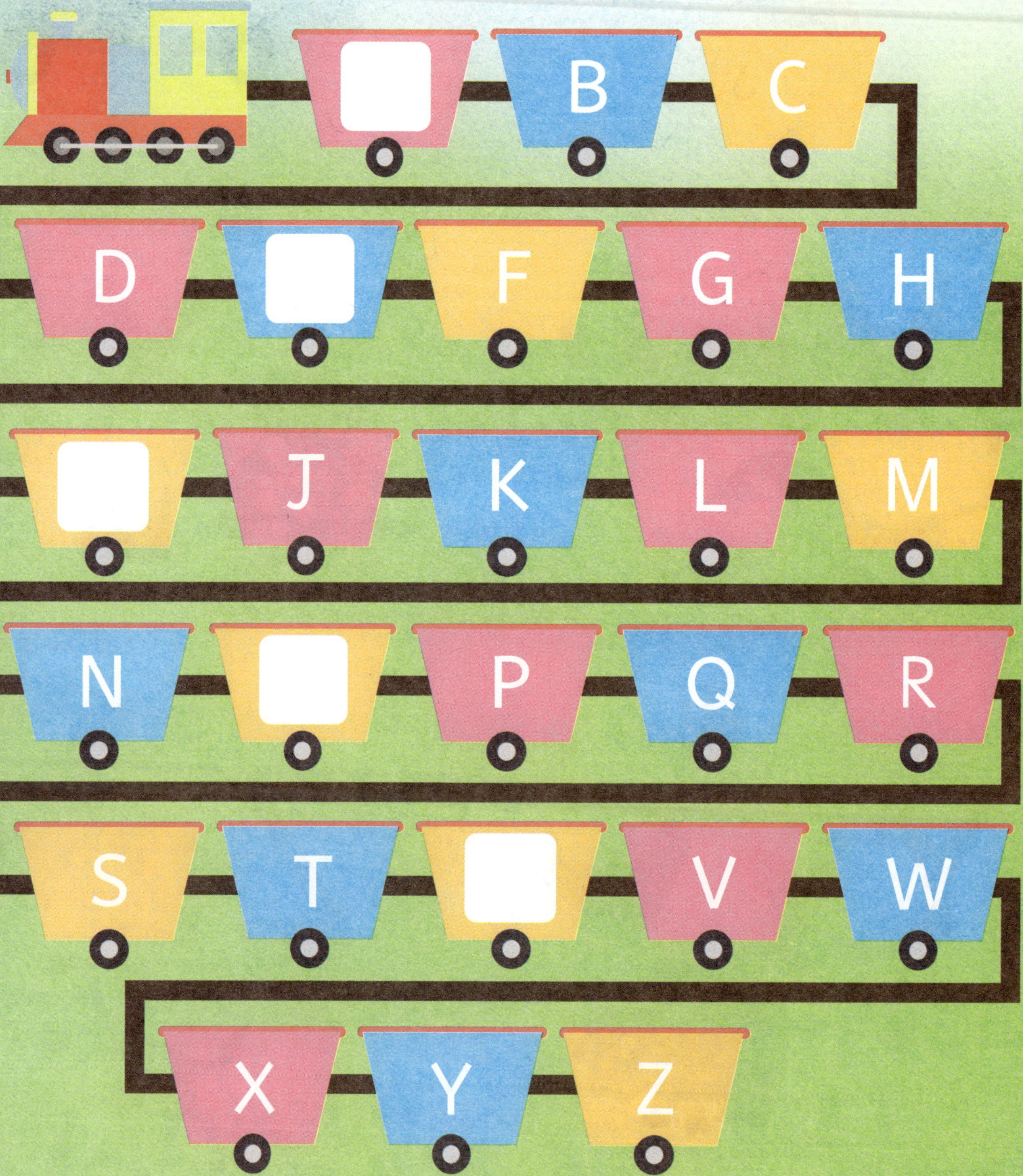

HELLO LETTERS
Aa and Bb

Read the words.

Trace and write a.

Read the words.

Trace and write b.

HELLO LETTERS Cc and Dd

Read the words.

Trace and write c.

c

Read the words.

Trace and write d.

d

I KNOW LETTERS Aa–Dd

Look at the pictures. Write the missing letters.

 _pple

 _oy

 _at

 _oll

 _ up

 _at

 _en

 _nt

Match the picture to the correct letter.

 • Aa • 

 • Bb • 

 • Cc • 

 • Dd • 

N O P Q R S T U V W X Y Z

HELLO LETTERS Ee and Ff

Read the words.

engine

eggplant

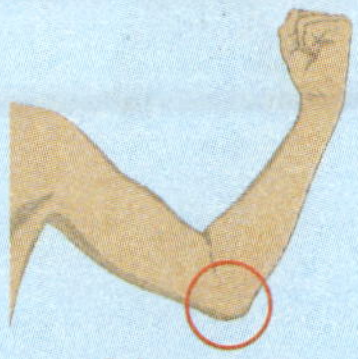
elbow

Ee

egg

elephant

Trace and write e.

e

Read the words.

fat

fog

fin

Ff

fun

fig

fan

Trace and write f.

f

HELLO LETTERS
Gg and Hh

Read the words.

Trace and write g.

g

Read the words.

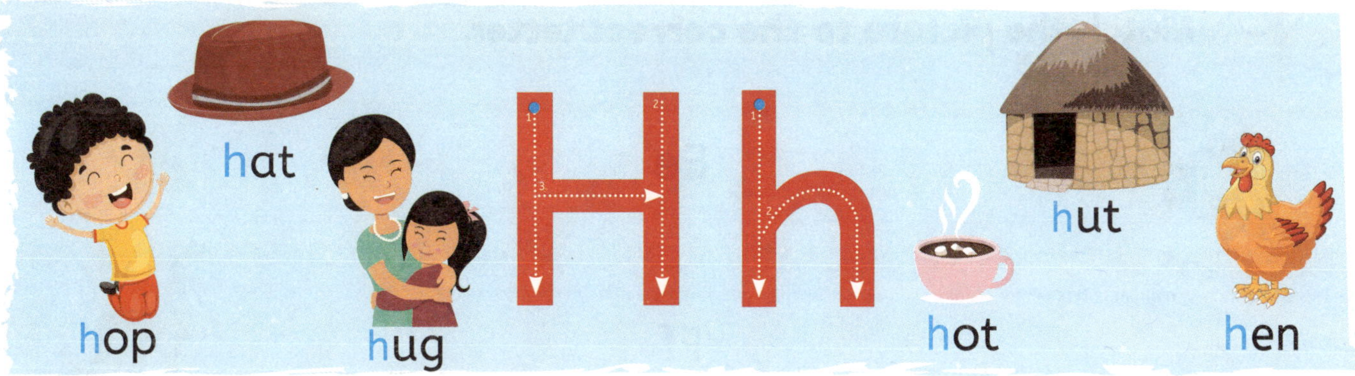

Trace and write h.

h

I KNOW LETTERS Ee–Hh

Look at the pictures. Write the missing letters.

 _ate

 _at

 _an

 _gg

 _en

 _ig

 _irl

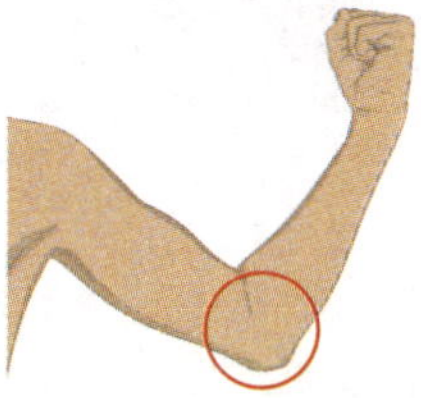 _lbow

Match the picture to the correct letter.

 Ee 

 Ff 

 Gg 

 Hh 

HELLO LETTERS Ii and Jj

Read the words.

India

ink

Ii

in

igloo

Trace and write i.

Read the words.

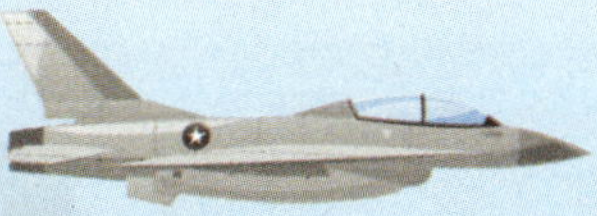
jet

jump

jog

Jj

jar

jam

Trace and write j.

HELLO LETTERS Kk and Ll

Read the words.

kettle

kitten

kangaroo

Kk

kite

king

Trace and write k.

k

Read the words.

lad

log

ladder

Ll

lip

lid

leg

lap

Trace and write l.

l

I KNOW LETTERS Ii–Ll

Look at the pictures. Write the missing letters.

_ing

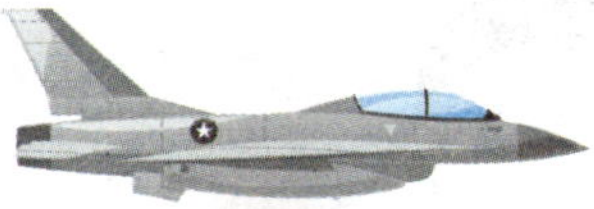

_et

_gloo

_ad

_og

_ite

_am

_nk

Match the picture to the correct letter.

Ii

Jj

Kk

Ll

HELLO LETTERS
Mm and Nn

Read the words.

Trace and write m.

m

Read the words.

Trace and write n.

n

HELLO LETTERS Oo and Pp

Read the words.

orange

octopus

otter

O o

ox

ostrich

Trace and write o.

o

Read the words.

pod

pup

pan

P p

pen

peg

pot

Trace and write p.

p

I KNOW LETTERS Mm–Pp

Look at the pictures. Write the missing letters.

 _en

 _ range

 _ap

 _up

 _x

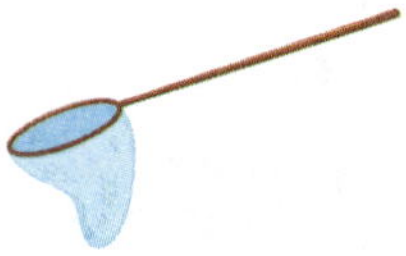 _et

 _ap

 _ug

Match the picture to the correct letter.

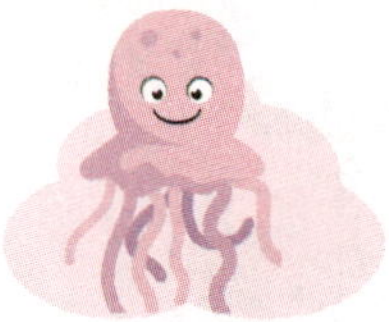

Mm

Nn

Oo

Pp

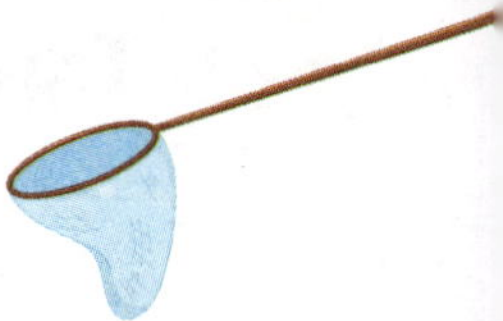

HELLO LETTERS Qq and Rr

Read the words.

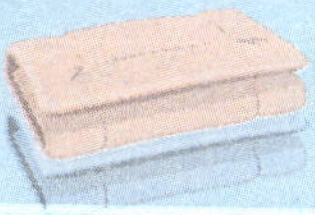
quilt

quiet

quail

queen

Trace and write q.

Read the words.

rug

rat

ram

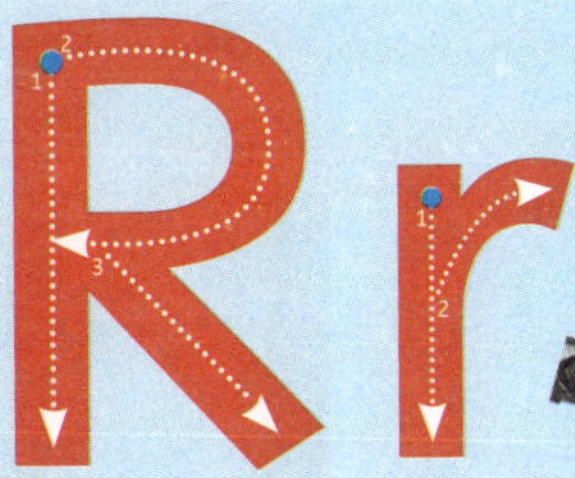

rag

rod

run

Trace and write r.

HELLO LETTERS Ss and Tt

Read the words.

Trace and write s.

Read the words.

Trace and write t.

I KNOW LETTERS Qq–Tt

Look at the pictures. Write the missing letters.

 _uiet

 _ing

 _ug

 _ip

 _op

 _od

 _ad

 _it

Match the pictures to the correct letters.

Qq

Rr

Ss

Tt

HELLO LETTERS Uu and Vv

Read the words.

umbrella

under

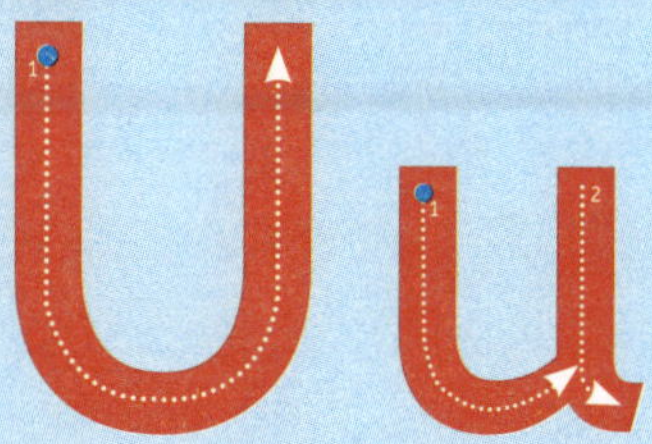

umpire

up

urn

Trace and write u.

u

Read the words.

vet

vulture

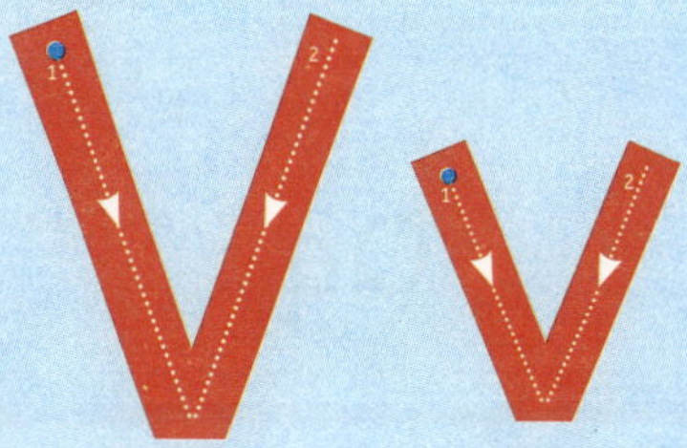

van

vase

Trace and write v.

v

HELLO LETTERS Ww and Xx

Read the words.

Trace and write w.

w

Read the words.

Trace and write x.

x

HELLO LETTERS Yy and Zz

Read the words.

Trace and write y.

y

Read the words.

Trace and write z.

z

I KNOW LETTERS Uu-Zz

Look at the pictures. Write the missing letters.

 _rn

 _ak

 _ip

 _an

 _ in

 _ero

 _mas

 _et

Match the picture to the correct letter.

	Uu	
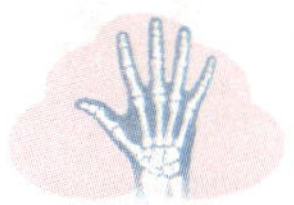	Vv	
	Ww	
	Xx	
	Yy	
	Zz	

N O P Q R S T U V W X Y Z

I KNOW THIS-THAT!

Look at the pictures. Circle the correct word.

this that

this that

this that

this that

Point and read. Circle the correct word.

What is  ?

This/That is a  .

What is  ?

This/That is the  .

What is  ?

This/That is a  .

What is  ?

This/That is a  .

Circle the correct picture.

That is an apple.

That is a bird.

This is a hat.

That is an ant.

This is a flower.

This is a star.

This is a house.

That is a car.

I KNOW WHERE YOU HIDE!

Read and draw.

cup on the 

cup under the 

Point and read. Trace the word.

Where is the  ?

It is between the  .

Where is the  ?

It is beside the  .

Match the picture to the correct group of words.

egg beside a pan

cat inside the box

hen under a tree

cup between jars

rat on a mat

INTRODUCTION TO ONE-MANY

Point and read.

add 's'

boy boys

add 's'
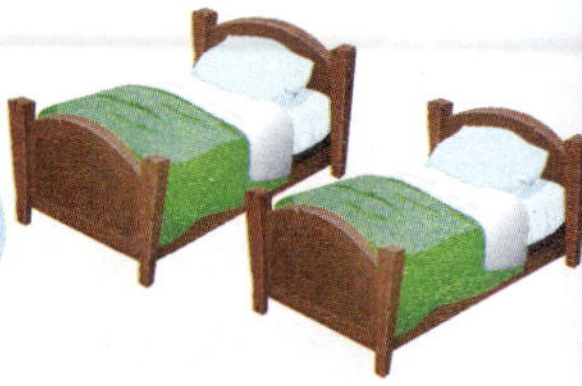

bed beds

Circle the correct word.

bat bats

hat hats

Match the pictures to the correct words.

eggs •		• egg
ant •		• ants
girls •		• girl

I KNOW ONE AND MANY THINGS!

Circle the correct word.

pup pups

top tops

map maps

boy boys

Read and draw.

one 

many 

Circle the correct word.

bat
bats

hat
hats

ball
balls

apple
apples

bear
bears

cup
cups

Read the words. Circle the correct picture.

stars

pumpkin

flowers

INTRODUCTION TO THESE-THOSE

Point and read.

this balloon

these balloons

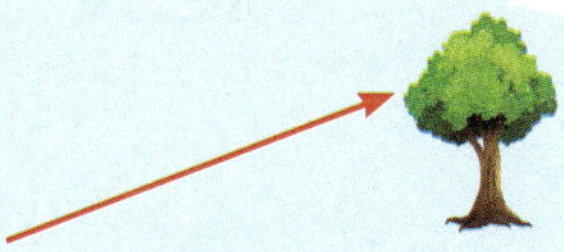

that tree

those trees

Look at these pictures. Circle the correct word.

these

this

that

those

these

this

that

those

I KNOW THESE–THOSE THINGS!

Circle the correct word.

that those

this these

that these

those these

Point and read. Trace the words.

What are  ?

Those are fans

What are ?

These are jars

Circle the correct picture.

Those are stars.

These are books.

These are bells.

Those are bees.

Choose the correct word.

these those

these those

these those

these those

I KNOW WHAT YOU DO!

Listen and cross out (×).

Touch the picture. Say the word.

cook

write

skate

jump

jog

run

cry

fly

share

Match the picture to the correct word.

sing

sleep

run

jump

read

DOBBY AND HIS FRIENDS

Look at the pictures. Talk about each picture.

Read about Dobby, Rob and Leena.

Hello! I am Dobby  .

I like to eat   and  .

This is Rob  .

 is my friend.

He likes to eat  and  .

He shares his treats with me.

This is Leena  .

She and  are friends.

She likes to eat  .

She gets  for me.

What do you like to eat? Draw here.

QUESTION WORDS

Colour the words. Use pencil colours.

Who What

Where

Point and read.

Who

about others around you

What

about things and objects

Where

about different places

Look at the picture. Read and answer.

Q. Who is this?
A. This is a boy.

Q. What is that?
A. That is the sun.

Q. Where is the cup?
A. The cup is on the table.

Match the picture to the correct question.

Who is this?	
Who is that?	
What is that?	
What is this?	
Where is the ball?	

I KNOW!

Circle the correct question word.

what	who	who	what	who	where

who	where	who	where	who	where

Circle the correct picture.

who

what

where

what

who

where

I KNOW SIGHT WORDS!

Point and read.

I	am	this	that	you	me
eat	are	we	mother	father	old
happy	soon	away	down	brown	up
black	can	come	find	get	new
uncle					

Read the sight words. Write them in the correct place on the wall.

is I up get mother away father am brown are uncle happy

READING WORDS (SHORT VOWEL 'a' WORDS)

Point and read.

-ab: cab tab

-ad: lad sad

-ag: bag rag tag

-an: fan pan

-ap: cap lap map tap

-at: bat cat hat rat

I KNOW!

Write the missing letter.

 c _ b

 l _ d

 f _ n

 b _ g

 c _ p

 b _ t

Join the letters to make words. Write the words.

t h a

r g a

n p a

t b a

d a s

g a t

t r a

p l a

m p a

I CAN WRITE WORDS!

Using the help box, write the names of the pictures.

lad hat man fan van pan rat sad cap

READING WORDS (SHORT VOWEL 'e' WORDS)

Point and read.

-ed: bed, red, wed

-eg: beg, leg, peg

-en: den, hen, pen, ten

-et: jet, net, vet, wet

I KNOW!

Write the missing letter.

b _ d

p _ g

j _ t

w _ d

d _ n

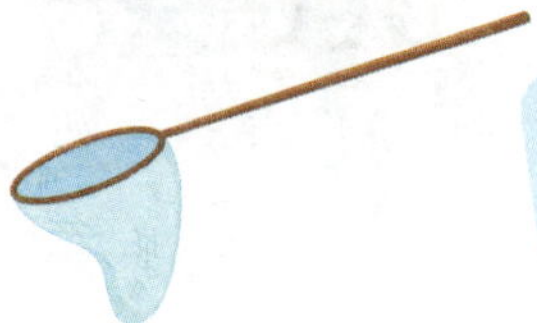

n _ t

Read the words. Circle the rhyming words.

vet	wet	cab
hen	tag	pen
leg	ant	beg
bed	red	peg

I CAN READ

Read these sentences.

Jen is my pet.

I pet Jen.

I let Jen get wet.

I met the vet.

I bet the vet can help.

Fill in the blanks.

wet vet pet

Jen is my ___________.

Jen is ___________.

I met the ___________.

READING WORDS (SHORT VOWEL 'i' WORDS)

Point and read.

-ib: bib, rib

-id: kid, lid

-ig: big, dig, fig

-in: bin, fin, pin, tin, win

-ip: hip, lip, sip, tip

-it: pit, sit, fit, kit, bit

I KNOW!

Write the missing letter.

 b _ b

 p _ t

 l _ d

 f _ g

 l _ p

 p _ n

Join the letters to make words. Write the words.

b b i	b r i	d i k
g i d	n b i	t n i
n w i	p i h	t p i

N O P Q R S T U V W X Y Z

I CAN WRITE WORDS!

Using the help box, write the names of the pictures.

jet tin vet peg den hen bin nib zip

READING WORDS (SHORT VOWEL 'o' WORDS)

Point and read.

-ob: sob, cob, hob

-od: nod, pod, rod, cod

-og: dog, fog, jog

-op: hop, mop, top, cop, pop

-ot: cot, dot, hot, not, pot

I KNOW!

Write the missing letter.

d _ t

m _ p

p _ d

c _ t

f _ g

d _ g

Read the words. Circle the rhyming words.

wet	dog	log
top	mop	vet
dot	lip	cot
tin	bin	map

I CAN WRITE WORDS!

Using the help box, write the names of the pictures.

bat top dot cot bed box sit pot rod

READING WORDS (SHORT VOWEL 'u' WORDS)

Point and read.

-ub: rub tub

-ud: bud mud

-ug: hug jug tug rug mug

-um: gum hum sum

-un: bun run fun sun

-up: cup pup

-ut: cut hut nut

-us: bus

I KNOW!

Write the missing letter.

 t _ b

 b _ n

 b _ d

 n _ t

 j _ g

 h _ t

Join the letters to make words. Write the words.

b r u

u d b

g u h

u m g

f n u

h t u

I CAN READ

Read these sentences.

Tim has a bug.

The bug sleeps in a mug.

The bug plays on a rug.

The bug fell into a jug.

Tim dug the bug out of the jug.

I CAN READ

Tick the correct answer.

Tim has a

jug ☐ rug ☐ bug ☐

The bug sleeps in a

jug ☐ rug ☐ mug ☐

The bug plays on a

jug ☐ rug ☐ bug ☐

Tim dug the bug out of the

jug ☐ rug ☐ bug ☐

INTRODUCTION TO A/AN

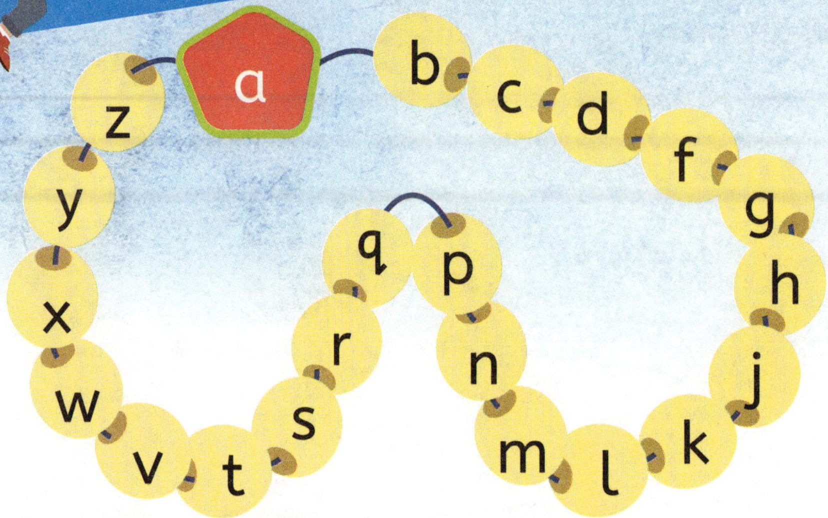

a comes before the sound of the letters:
b, c, d, f, g, h, j, k, l, m, n, p, q, r, s, t, v, w, x, y, z

an comes before the sound of the letters:
a, e, i, o, u

Name the pictures. Circle the correct word.

a an

a an

a an

a an

a an

a an

Look at the pictures. Name them. Write a/an before them. One has been done for you.

an   

MAGIC 'e'

Sing.

Let me teach you a game
Magic e is my name
Add me to any word...
abracadabra...
Hear the vowel say its name.

Name the pictures. Add the magic e. Read the words.

tap + e
↓
tape 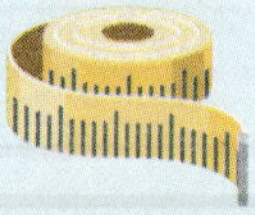

fin + e
↓
fine 

tub + e
↓
tube 

bit + e
↓
bite 

can + e
↓
cane 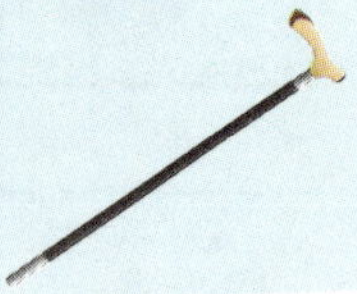

man + e
↓
mane 

Add the magic e and write the new word.
Match the words to the pictures.

tap ____________ • 

cub ____________ • 

tub ____________ • 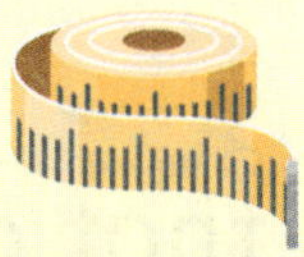

kit ____________ • 

pan ____________ • 

mat ____________ • 

plan ____________ • 

INTRODUCTION TO YES/NO

Circle Yes or No.

Is this a hat?  Yes / No

Is that a net? 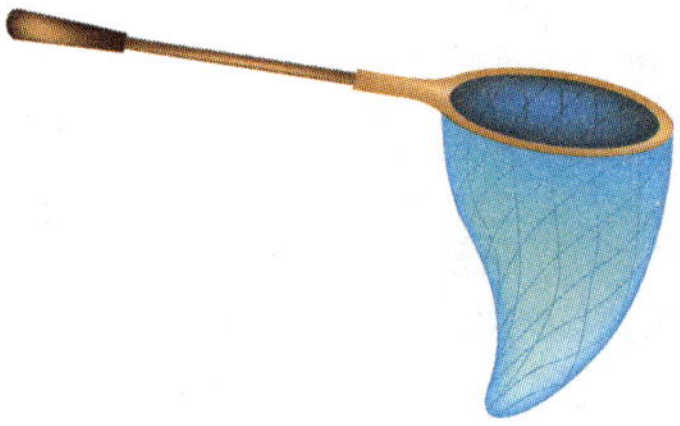 Yes / No

Is this a bib?  Yes / No

Is that a mug?  Yes / No

Is this a tub?  Yes / No

Listen and write only Yes/No in the space given.

Can a fish swim?

Can an elephant fly?

Can a dog wag its tail?

Can bees make honey?

READING MORE WORDS

Point and read.

train

paint

rain

sail

mail

chain

play

pray

tray

say

hay

day

READING MORE WORDS

Point and read.

evening

equal

eat

treat

sea

easy

tea

clean

read

leaf

bean

neat

READING MORE WORDS

Point and read.

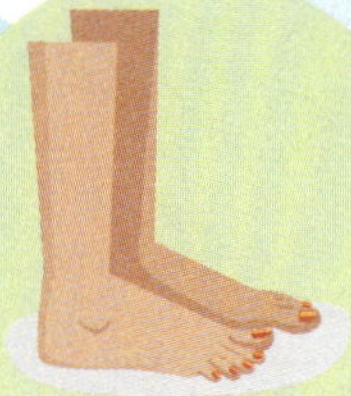
feet

bee

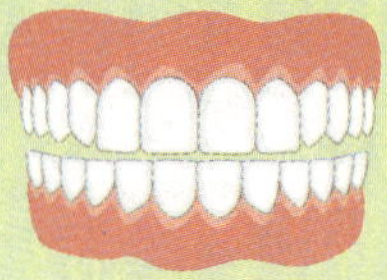
teeth

tree

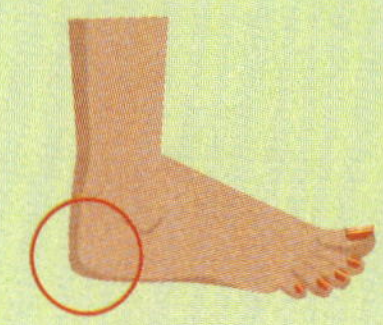
heel

field

thief

baby

windy

shiny

tidy

party

READING MORE WORDS

Point and read.

ice cream

item

iron

light

night

right

tight

tie

pie

dry

cry

fry

fly

READING MORE WORDS

Point and read.

no

go

so

soap

goat

toast

coat

road

arrow

crow

slow

low

grow

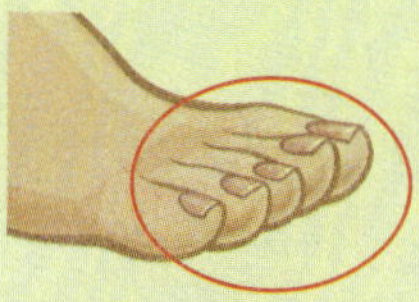

toes

READING MORE WORDS

Point and read.

uniform

utensil

unicorn

new

news

few

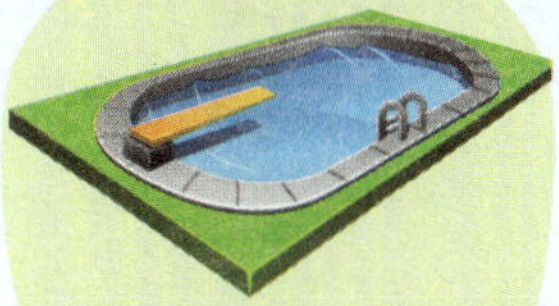

pool

room

food

school

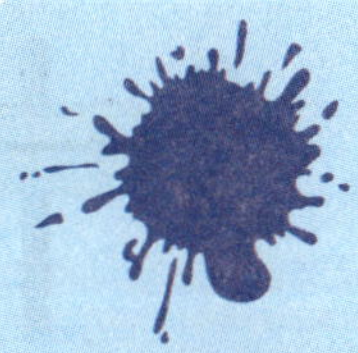

blue

glue

I KNOW!

Fill in the missing letters.

ai, ay

tr .... n

r .... n

tr ....

ee, y

b ....

tr ....

bab........

ea

tr .... t

cl .... n

igh, y

n .... t

cr ....

oo, ue

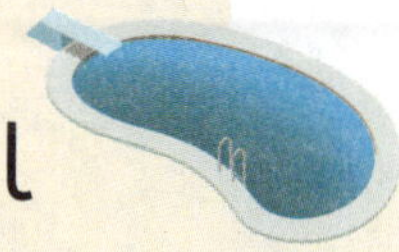

p l

sch l

bl ....

oa, o

g .... t

r .... d

g ....

I KNOW!

Read the words. Cross (×) the odd one out. One has been done for you.

play	day	hay	cry
rain	train	cake	paint
night	fly	right	tight
pool	school	food	top
goat	coat	road	iron
dry	cry	fry	party

Name the picture. Read the words. Circle the rhyming word.

rain

arrow

feet

iron

tiny

ink

day

ant

neat

egg

blue

under

I KNOW!

Write the beginning letter of each word.
Write the new word!

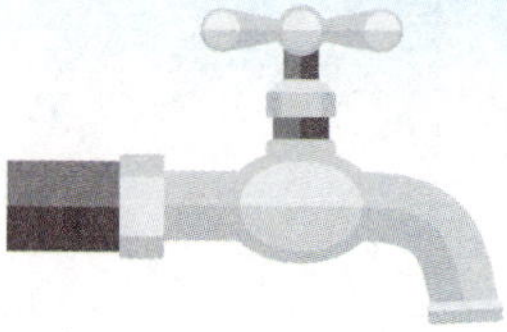  

I KNOW!

Write the beginning letter of each word.
Write the new word!

 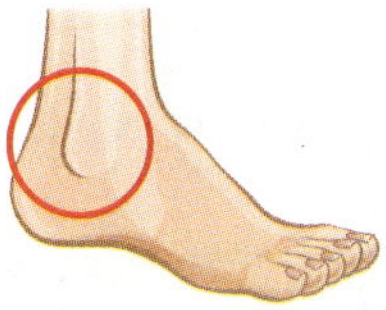  

INTRODUCTION TO AND

And is used to join two words.

 and 

apple and mango

apple and mango

 and 

bread and butter

bread and butter

 and 

dog and cat

dog and cat

 and 

lock and key

lock and key

There is a  and a  on the table.

book bag

There is a book and a bag on the table.

 and  are vegetables.

Pumpkin carrot

Pumpkin and carrot are vegetables.

Read and paste the correct sticker and trace 'and' to complete the sentence

There is a bat 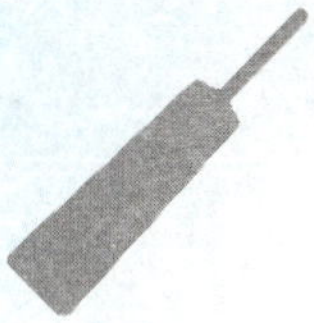 and a ball .

There is a pen  and a cup  on the table.

I saw a deer  and a lion  in the zoo.

We have two hands   and two legs .

Bob loves to read  and write .

Join the two words using 'and'.

day

night ______________________________

ball

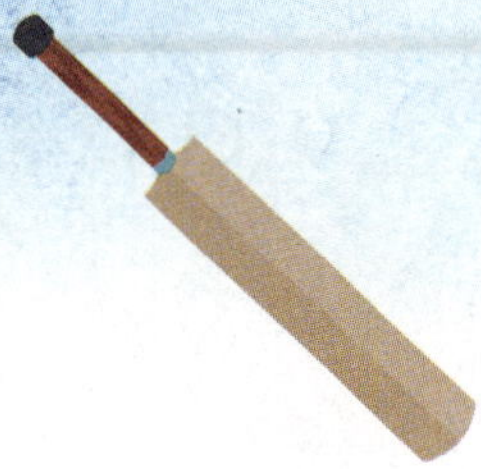

bat ______________________________

shoes

socks ______________________________

bird

nest ______________________________

paper

pen ______________________________

THE FOX AND THE CRANE

Listen to the story. Draw and colour to complete the pictures.

At the fox's home

At the crane's home

I CAN READ!

Point and read.

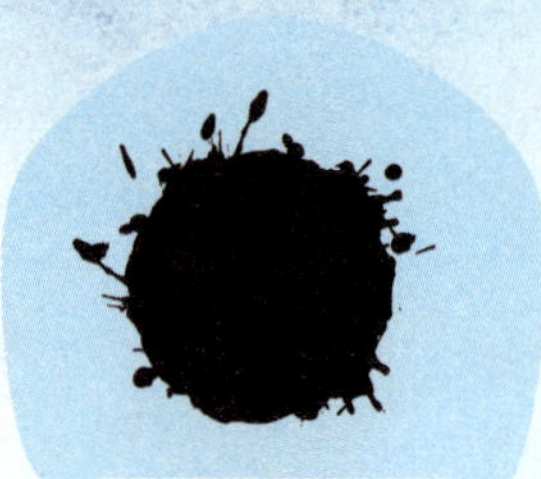

black

blossom

block

floor

flag

fly

plant

plug

plate

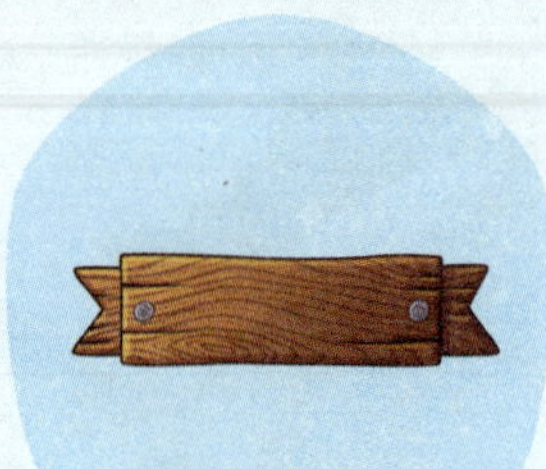

plank

I CAN READ!

Point and read.

brush

bread

brick

draw

drink

drum

fry

frock

grass

green

grapes

glass

I CAN READ!

Point and read.

crow

cross

crab

crane

class

clown

clove

clay

small

smell

smile

write

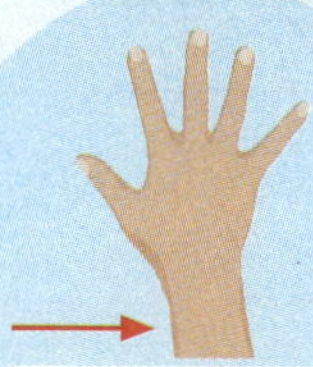

wrist

wrong

I CAN READ!

Point and read.

spin

spot

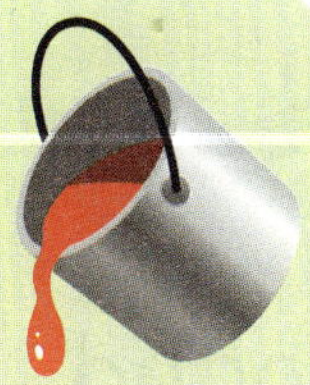
spill

snake

snail

sneeze

step

stop

star

store

I CAN READ!

Point and read.

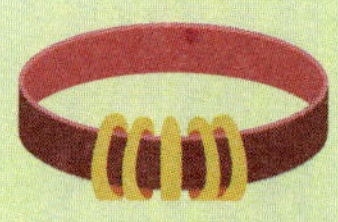

band

sand

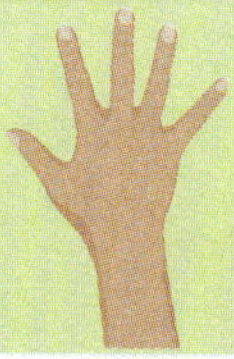

hand

sing

king

ring

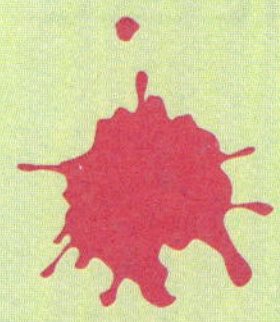

pink

sink

link

whisk

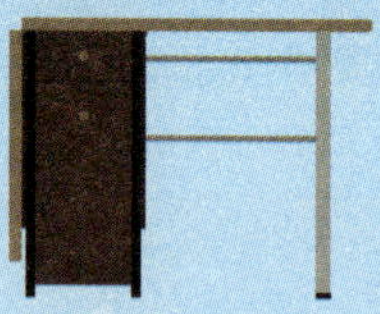

desk

mask

I CAN READ!

Point and read.

chair

chain

chips

chirp

ship

shell

shoes

shorts

share

shirt

shape

shelf

shop

I CAN READ!

Point and read.

wheel

whale

white

whisk

thick

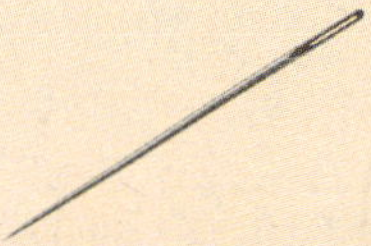
thin

thumb

this
that
these
those

they
them

why
when
where
what

I KNOW!

Circle the correct sound.

bl fl

pl fl

pl bl

br bl

gr gl

sh sn

sn sp

st sn

sh sp

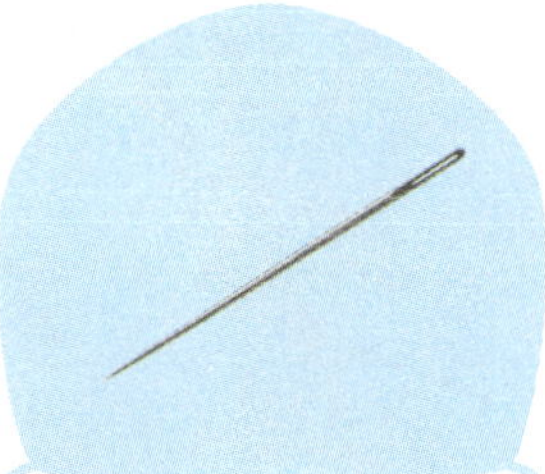
thin this

cl gl

sh sm

I KNOW!

Circle the correct sound.

ng nk

ng nk

t th

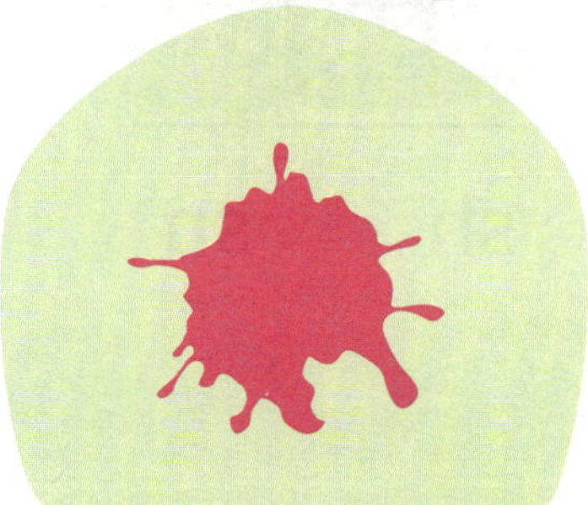

nk ng

ch sh

wh wr

sk sh

wh w

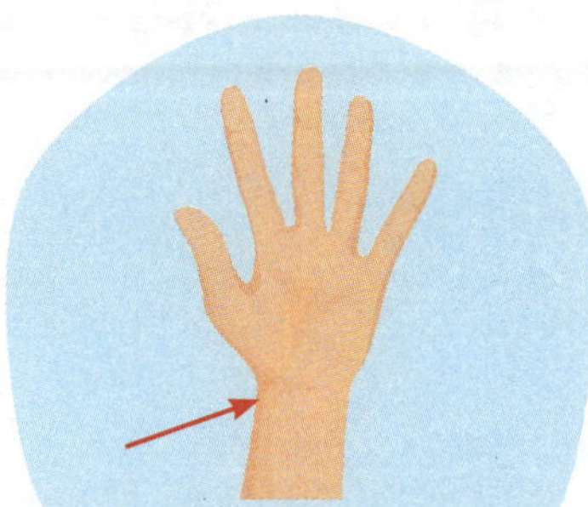

wr wh

I KNOW!

Write the missing letters. Read the words.

.............ack

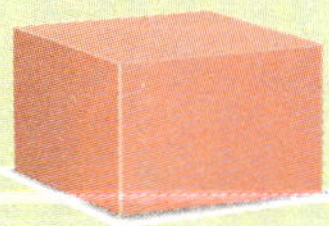

.............ock

.............ant

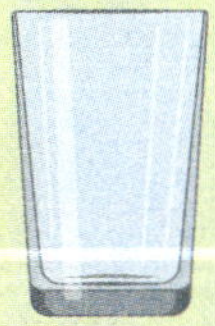

.............ass

.............een

.............um

.............own

.............ile

.............apes

.............ar

.............ot

ri.............

.............eel

.............ale

.............ain

.............ell

OPPOSITES

Point and read.

big

small

thin

thick

dirty

clean

cold

hot

open

close

empty

full

old

young

bad

good

happy

sad

day

night

Match the opposites.

Circle the opposite word.

thick small

young sad

thin small

I CAN READ (REPEATED CONSONANTS)

Point and read.

-all

ball

small

fall

tall

-ill

ill

pill
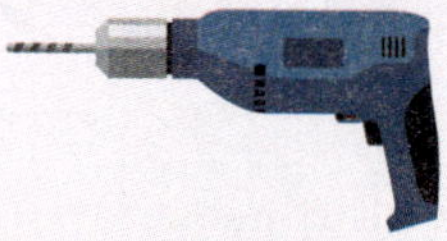
drill

bill

-ell

bell

tell

yellow

-oll

roll

-ull

bull

-ss

grass
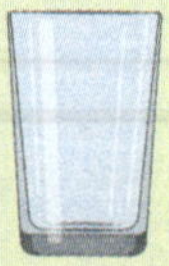
glass
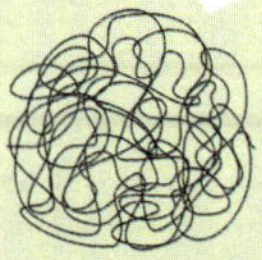
mess

kiss

-rr

cherry

strawberry

LAZY TOM

Look at these pictures. Talk about the pictures. Listen to the story.

I KNOW!

Write the missing letter.

lo _ _ ipop

i _ _

ki _ _

ta _ _

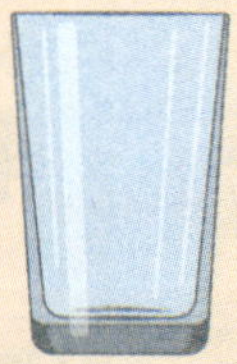

gla _ _

be _ _

je _ _ y

che _ _ y

I KNOW!

Point and read. Write the missing letter 2 times.

bu _ _ er

pu _ _ y

a _ _ le

he _ _ o

bu _ _ y

ki _ _ en

ba _ _ oon

do _ _

so _ _ y

I KNOW!

Circle the correct sound.

bl br

pl bl

sh sn

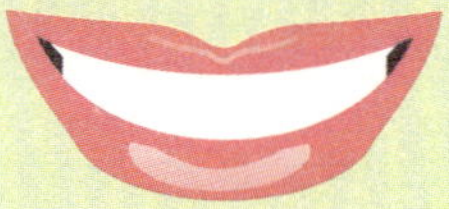

sm sn

st sp

ch sh

cl ch

wr wh

tr th

bl br

dr br

wh wr

I KNOW!

Read the words. Write them in the correct ladder.

chair	why	wheel
chop	shell	shop
shelf	chip	when

sh-

ch-

wh-

I KNOW!

Read the words. Write them in the correct ladder.

sneeze	brave	brush
snake	grass	green
grapes	brick	snail

sn-

gr-

br-

I KNOW!

Read the words. Write them in the correct group.

glass roll kiss tell bell mess

-ll

roll

-ss

glass

Write a/an below each picture.

RHYME ALONG

Circle the rhyming words.

day	say	cake
rain	train	man
eat	neat	tape
bean	clean	snake
sink	blink	iron
tree	fry	cry
coat	ox	boat
nest	slow	crow
pool	fool	hot

I KNOW!

Say the name of each picture. Cross (×) the odd one out.

GOLDILOCKS AND THE THREE BEARS

Look at the pictures. What do you think happens in the story? Listen to the story.

JUMBLED WORDS

Look at the pictures. Write their names.

p i sh

m dr u

t igh n

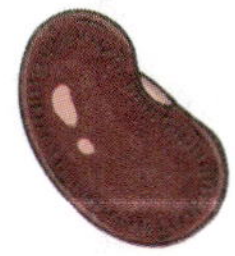

b n ea

ai r n

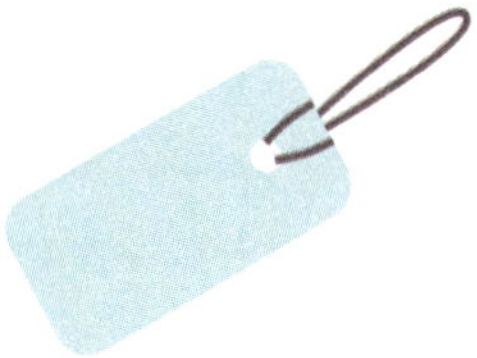

g t a

ew n s

ch p i s

JUMBLED WORDS

Look at the pictures. Write the correct spellings.

erte

wcro

aybb

eack

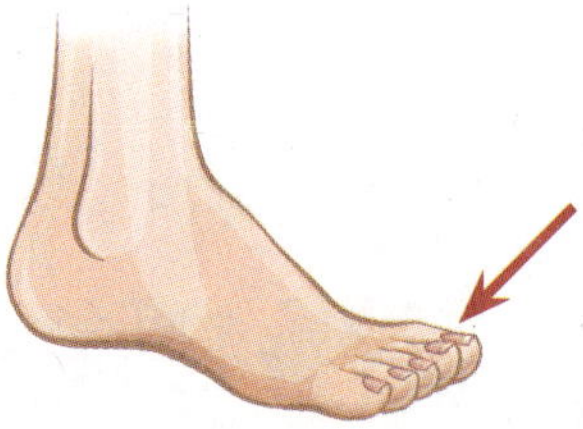

oet

moor

uelb

gkin

lehsl

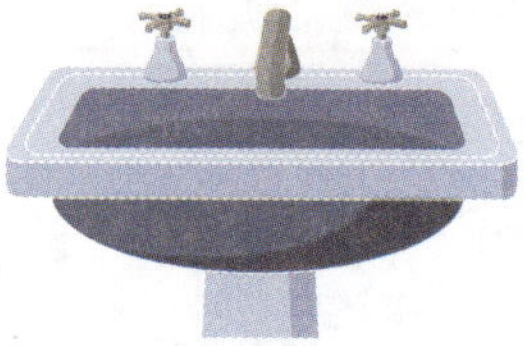

nksi

INTRODUCTION TO SENTENCES

Point and read.

Riya is a girl.

Ken is a boy.

Sam is a fat cat.

This is a red doll.

Riya is a girl. ← This is a sentence.

A sentence

- Starts with a capital letter
- Ends with a full stop
- Tells us something about objects, places and animals.
- The, It, That, These, This, Those

GUIDED SENTENCE WRITING

Read these sentences.

The cup is big.

I am Ria.

This is my dog.

The flower is pink.

Look at the pictures. Trace the sentences.

The mango is yellow.

This dress is blue.

This horse is black.

The box is big.

GUIDED SENTENCE WRITING YES/NO

Answer the following questions with Yes/No and complete the sentence.

Is this a book?

_____, this is not a book.

Is this a tree?

_____, this is a tree.

Is that a bus?

_____, that is not a bus.

Is this a chair?

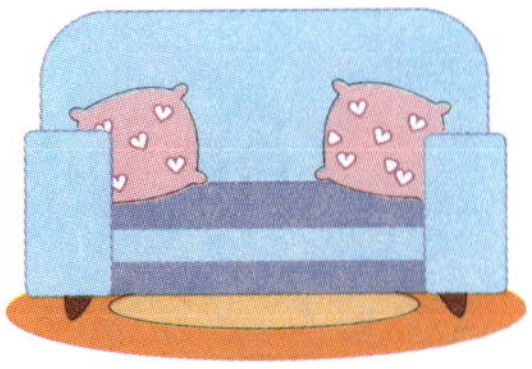

_____, this is not a chair.

Is this a bell?

_____, this is a bell.

GUIDED SENTENCE WRITING

Look at the pictures. Read the words. Complete the sentence about the picture.

is empty

The jug ______________________

______________________________.

is on the mat

The cat ______________________

______________________________.

is in the garden

Granny ______________________

______________________________.

is in the class

The boy ______________________

______________________________.

is singing

The girl ______________________

______________________________.

GUIDED SENTENCE WRITING

Look at the pictures. Write a sentence about each picture.

This is a ball.

This .

This .

This .

This .

This .

I CAN READ AND WRITE

Read these sentences.

My pets are at the vet.

There are three pets at the vet.

A cat, a dog and a fish are my pets.

Choose the correct answer.

Where are my pets?

at the house ☐ at the vet ☐ at the park ☐

Which one is not my pet? Circle it.

I CAN READ AND WRITE

Read these sentences.

I see a tree.

It has apples on it.

The apples are red.

I like to eat apples.

Answer these questions.

What do you see?

I see a ________________________.

What is on the tree? ________________________

What colour are the apples?

red blue black

I CAN READ AND WRITE

Read these sentences.

I see a bird.

She sits in her nest.

The nest has eggs.

I see three eggs.

Do you see eggs?

Answer these questions.

What do you see?

I see a ______________________.

Where does the bird sit?

The bird sits in her ______________________.

What is in the nest?

There are ______________________ in the nest.

How many eggs are there in the nest?

There are ______________________ eggs in the nest.

Sticker Page

Page 85:

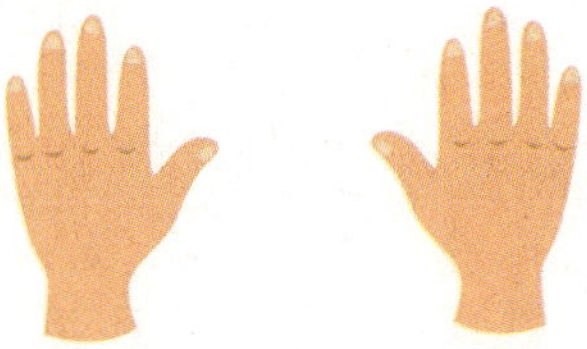